Walk and Explore

Myste

GW01417683

Dorset

by Robert Hesketh

Inspiring Places Publishing
2 Down Lodge Close
Alderholt
Fordingbridge
Hants
SP6 3JA

www.inspiringplaces.co.uk
ISBN 978-0-9955964-8-1

© Robert Hesketh 2021
www.roberthesketh.co.uk

Contains Ordnance Survey data © Crown copyright and database right (2011)

JURASSICCOAST
QUALITY
BUSINESS

Contents

Sandford Orcas Manor (page 17).

Introduction

Dorset's Jurassic Coast, rolling hills and chalk downs give wonderfully varied walking. The county is also rich in mystery and legend. Read on to discover the origin of the red signpost at Winterborne Tomson; the folklore of Lyme's marvellous fossils and how Satan cast the Agglestone onto Godlingston Heath.

Legend surrounds the white hart at King's Stag and T.E. Lawrence's untimely death at Cloud's Hill. Ghosts are legion in Dorset: animals are terrified by Eggardon's hillfort; ghostly armies clash at Badbury Rings and a phantom horseman menaces travellers near Sixpenny Handley. Bettiscombe has a screaming skull, Lulworth and Durdle Door their phantom dancers, Ashmore its unearthly "gabbygammies". Eastbury House at Tarrant Gunville is haunted by a wicked steward who shot himself on hearing of his master's return…and shoots himself again and again on a regular basis. Athelhampton House has several spirits, including two 17th century gentlemen who fight a duel. Sandford Orcas Manor trumps them all, with fourteen resident spirits.

Boots on? Time to go….These routes differ in length and terrain, so the time needed to complete will vary. But why hurry? Each walk has its own character with many viewpoints and places of interest. Please go at your own pace and I'm sure you'll enjoy them as much as I have.

Below: Looking east from Lyme Regis.

Clothing and Footwear - Exploring Dorset on foot is a pleasure throughout the seasons – so long as you're prepared. Mud, puddles and some rough footing are par for the course; good footwear is recommended.

The climate's (usually!) mild, but changeable. Pack waterproofs and an extra warm layer in your rucksack. Gorse and nettles often make trousers a better option than shorts, especially as they provide some protection from ticks, which may carry Lyme disease. If a tick does latch onto you, remove it carefully and promptly with tweezers.

Kit - Drinking water is essential. Walking poles or a stick are a great bonus, ditto extra food and a mobile phone. Use the book's sketch maps as a general guide, but Ordnance Survey Explorer maps for detail. Explorers 116, 117, 118, 129 and OL15 cover all the routes in this book. Bring a compass if you have one or have one on your phone.

The Countryside - Please remember most cliff paths are unfenced and mind out for uneven and waterlogged ground. Follow the Country Code; use field edges when crossing land with growing crops and leave gates closed or open as you find them. Keep dogs under control, particularly during the lambing and bird nesting seasons.

Public Transport - Check www.travelinesw.com (01872 510028) for the latest information.

Starting Points and others are given as accurate map references. If you have a smart phone it's a good idea to get an app which gives grid references (many are free) to check your location.

Tolpuddle, the Martyrs' Shelter.

Lyme Regis - *fossil legends*

Distance: 3¼ miles/5.1km Time: 2 hours Grade: Easy

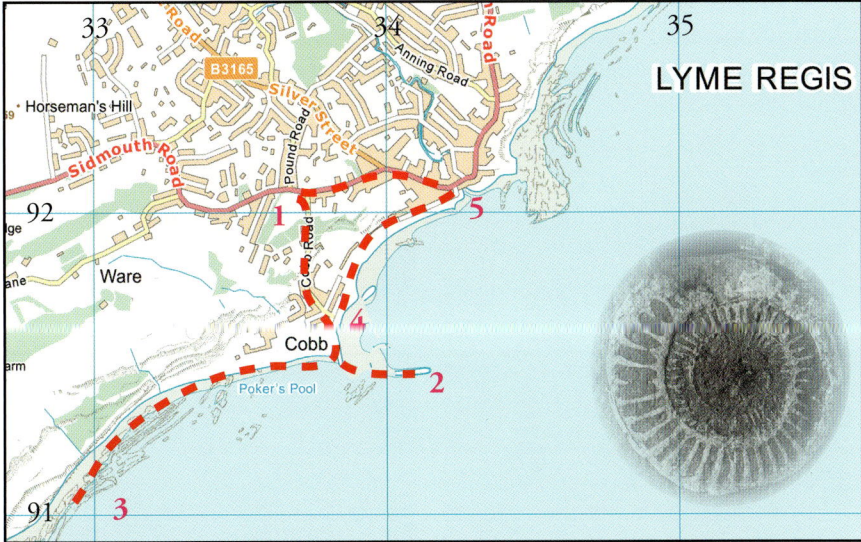

Start/parking: Holmbush car park, Pound Street SY33713 92080. DT7 3HX.
Refreshments: Wide choice of cafés, pubs and restaurants.
Terrain: Tarred paths and streets. One moderately long ascent and descent.
Stiles: 0
Public Toilets: At start and on seafront.
Maps: Explorer 116 or Landranger 193.

1.　　　**Start SY33713 92080** from the car park entrance. Walk past the café. Turn left down steps. Follow the lane downhill. Continue past the Lifeboat Station to explore the Cobb, Lyme's sinuous breakwater, which dates from the 14th century.

2.　　　**½ mile/0.9km SY34034 91475:** Reaching the end of the Cobb, retrace your steps. Turn left at the Lifeboat Station. Walk through the car park. Turn left to Monmouth Beach. The more dramatic fossil exposures are further west along the beach, from SY33084 91018 onwards. Explore the limestone boulders as well as the pavement. Low tide also reveals many rock pools.

3.　　　**1½ miles/2.5km SY32855 91025:** Retrace your steps along the beach when you reach the end of the ammonite pavement.

4.　　　**2½ miles/3.8km SY33803 91638:** From the Lifeboat Station follow the Esplanade around Cobb Gate Beach into Marine Parade, with its attractive medley of historic buildings. At the far end of the Walk is a plaque commemorating Lyme's role in D Day, 1944.

5.   **2¾ miles/4.5km SY34237 92071:** Reaching the Town Clock, turn right into Broad Street to visit the Fossil Shop and Lyme Regis Museum. Turn around and retrace your steps along Broad Street and thence uphill. On the way are several handsome buildings, mainly early 19th century. Divert right into Drake's Way for the Fossil Workshop. Continue up Broad Street past the Forge Fossil Shop. When the road forks, keep left. Continue to the start.

Clockwise from top left: The famous harbour wall known as the Cobb; Monmouth Beach; an ammonite from Monmouth Beach; Gryphea, an ancient mollusc.

Lyme Regis has been a deservedly popular resort since Georgian times. Nestling beneath the rugged cliffs that ring Lyme Bay, it has many buildings from that period that would be instantly recognizable to the characters from Jane Austen's novel *Persuasion* and John Fowles' *The French Lieutenant's Woman*, both of which have been filmed in and around the town.

Dorset's Jurassic Coast is noted for fossils and Lyme has a particularly rich fossil heritage. Allow extra time to visit Lyme's excellent museum and fossil shops and to explore the fossil exposures on Monmouth Beach, where low tide reveals a fascinating array of ammonites in the ammonite pavement and boulders.

Before fossilization and evolution were understood, fossils were explained through a rich assortment of folk tales, reflected in their popular names. Ammonites, extinct sea dwelling cephalopod molluscs, were known as "snakestones", and were said to be coiled snakes, conger eels or monstrous sea serpents that had lost their heads. By association, snakestones were carried as protection against snake bite in the same way adder fat was used in Dorset to cure the effects of snake bite.

"Thunderbolts" or "Thunder Bullets" are the Dorset names for the slender bullet shaped fossils said to have been thrown down from the heavens during thunderstorms. Very common on the beaches of Lyme and Charmouth they are belomnites, fossilized parts of a cuttlefish that, like ammonites, died out at the end of the Cretaceous Period, 66 million years ago.

"Devil's toenails" is the popular name for the gnarled, curved fossilized shells of Gryphea, an extinct oyster, whilst "Fairy Loaves" are the small heart shaped fossilized shells of a prehistoric sea urchin. It was believed they were baked by fairies and imbued with magic. Fairy Loaves ensured a house would never be without bread, whilst milk kept by them would not sour.

Please visit at low tide, stay well clear of the notoriously unstable cliffs and beware of slippery, uneven rocks and the returning tide. Several fossil hunting expeditions are organized by experienced collectors. (Tide times are available from Lyme TIC 01297 442138 and the internet.)

Lyme Regis from the Cobb.

Seatown and Golden Cap - *the haunted Anchor Inn*

Distance: 2½ miles/3.9km Time: 1½ hours Grade: Moderate

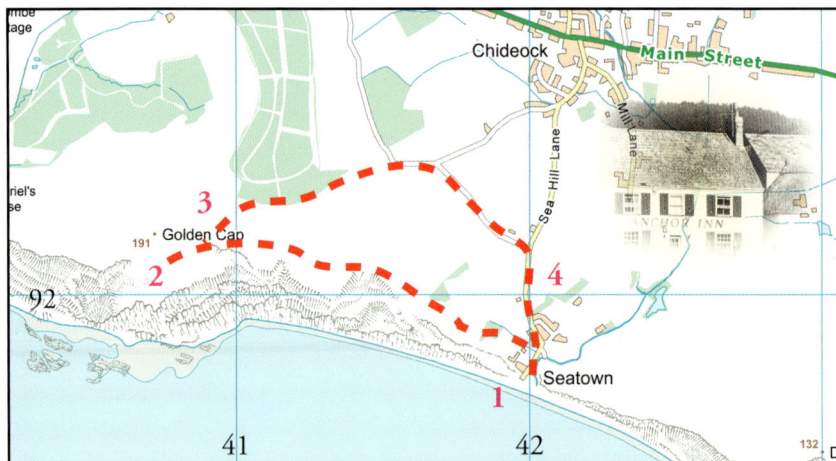

Start/parking: Car park opposite Anchor Inn, Seatown, SY42067 91755, DT6 6JU.

Terrain: Signed Coastpath; footpath; quiet lane. One long ascent and descent.

Refreshments: Anchor Inn, 01297 489215.

Stiles: 0

Public Toilets: At start.

Maps: OS Explorer OL116, Landranger 193.

1.   **Start SY42067 91755:** Turn right up the lane for 200m. Turn left at the Coastpath sign.   Keep ahead at a crosstracks "Golden Cap". Continue uphill on the well-beaten path. Enjoy the views from the triangulation pillar on the summit, and then continue over the level path to enjoy the equally stunning views westwards.

2.   **1¼ miles/1.8km SY40547 92132:** You may simply retrace your steps to the start, or make a circular walk along Pettycrate Lane as follows. Retrace your steps to the triangulation pillar. Continue down the stepped path for 150m to a path division and signpost.

3.   **1¼ miles/2km SY40787 92270:** Fork left "Langdon Hill and Car Park". Continue ahead "Chideock and Seatown" at the next two crosstracks. At a third crosstrack, continue ahead "Seatown" between hedges. Keep right when the path next forks. Continue to a lane.

4.   **2¼ miles/3.4km SY41998 92160:** Turn right and follow the lane to the start.

Golden Cap, the highlight of this classic coastal walk, is a massive cliff of lias, Jurassic clays and mudstones. Capped with a golden crown of Cretaceous greensand it stands 630ft (191m) above the sea and is the highest and most impressive peak on England's south coast. The views are magnificent: look east along the 18 mile stretch of Chesil Bank to Portland Bill and westwards across the broad sweep of Lyme Bay to Torbay. Afterwards, enjoy refreshment at the Anchor Inn and explore Seatown's 1¼ mile long shingle beach. Fossil hunting is best at low tide. Swimming is possible, but please heed warnings of tides and currents and keep clear of the unstable cliffs.

The Haunted Anchor Inn

Seatown's Anchor Inn has a huge collection of local photographs, both period and contemporary, plus fossils and items recovered from shipwrecks. It overlooks the beach where many cargoes of contraband were landed in the 18th and early 19th centuries. Aware of the extent of smuggling hereabouts, the government stationed an exciseman nearby from 1750. In this close knit community many were deeply involved in the "Free Trade" and excisemen were deeply resented.

One exciseman was shot dead at the top of the Anchor's stairs as he eavesdropped on a gang of smugglers below. His ghost is said to haunt the inn and the neighbouring thatched cottage.

The view east from Golden Cap.

Bettiscombe Manor - *the Screaming Skull*

Distance: 6 miles/9.6km Time: 3 hours   Grade: Moderate

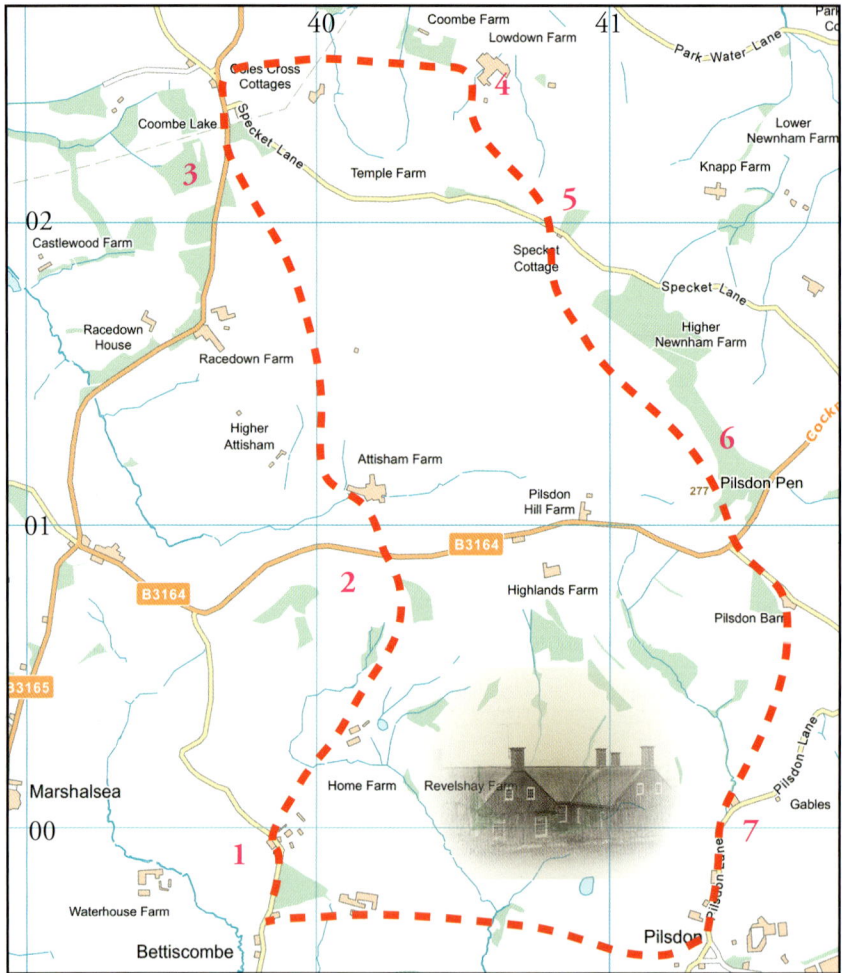

Start/parking: Bettiscombe village hall car park, ST399000 Postcode DT6 5NT.

Terrain: Footpaths, bridlepaths, short lane and road sections. Some short, steep ascents. One wet area near Point 5. Path signing is incomplete: attention to map and directions needed.

Stiles: 6 **Refreshments:** None en route. Nearby, Bottle Inn, Marshwood and Shave Cross Inn.

Public Toilets: None. **Maps:** Ordnance Survey Explorer 116; Landranger 193.

1.   **Start ST399 000:** Turn right out of the car park. Follow the bridleway for 400m. Reaching Bettiscombe Manor, turn left. Follow the brick wall right around the back of the house. Keep the hedge on your right. Walk uphill. Exit by a field gate. Continue steeply uphill as signed.

2.   **¾ mile/1km ST402 009:** Cross the lane. Follow the track ahead past Attisham Farm. At the track junction, turn left for 50m. Bear right uphill. Continue ahead at the next path junction.

3.   **1¾ miles/2.6km ST397 022:** Reaching the road, continue ahead past the village hall. Ignore the lane on the right. Turn right over stile, signed "Whitham Mill Cross". Continue with the field edge on your right. Cross another stile. Continue east to a footbridge. Cross, turn left into a coppice. The path continues just left of buildings.

4.   **2¼ miles/3.7km ST405 026:** Turn right at the Jubilee Trail sign. The path divides at the next gate. Turn right on the Jubilee Trail. Follow the path just to the right of houses, then uphill. Bear left at a cattle grid. Continue diagonally left uphill along a line of pylons and on through bracken.

5.   **3 miles/4.6km ST408 020:** Reaching a lane, continue ahead up steps for "Pilsdon Pen". The path climbs steeply to the top gate. Cross a field. Exit by a pair of gates. Bear diagonally right across the next field to a gate. Follow the track down to the next gate. Bear left over a stile onto Pilsdon Pen. Climb diagonally uphill to explore the ramparts.

6.   **3¾ miles/5.8km ST414 012:** Take the path left of the triangulation pillar downhill to the road. Take the lane ahead "Pilsdon Shave Cross". After 250m, turn right through a small gate by a tennis court. Follow signs around the house. Continue over a stile, downhill to a lane.

7.   **4½ miles/7.1km ST414 001:** Turn right for 400m. Turn right onto a signed footpath (no vehicular access) opposite the lane to Pilsdon Dairy. Continue ahead on the farm track at the next path junction. Walk past Lower House Farm to a lane. Turn right to the start.

The view south from Pilsdon Pen.

This pleasing circuit through green fields and rolling hills passes around Bettiscombe Manor (please respect the owners' privacy). It includes Pilsdon Pen, (909ft /277m), the second highest hill in Dorset, with views south to Golden Cap and the Channel; west to Dartmoor and the Quantocks and north to the Polden and Mendip hills. Pilsdon Pen is topped by the ramparts of an Iron Age hillfort, one of several concentrated on the Dorset/Devon border built by the Durotiges, the Celtic tribe who gave their name to Dorset. A complementary group of Iron Age hillforts built by the Dumnonni (who gave their name to Devon) are found in East Devon. Pilsdon Pen's steep slopes formed a natural defence, fortified with two massive ramparts, ditches and wooden palisades.

Pilsdon Pen.

John Symonds Udal (see bibliography) first recorded Bettiscombe Manor's skull in 1872: "At a farmhouse in Dorsetshire is carefully preserved a human skull, which has been there for a period long antecedent to the present tenancy. The peculiar superstition attaching to it is that if it be brought out of the house, the house itself would rock to its foundations, whilst the person by whom such an act of desecration was committed would certainly die within the year. It is strangely suggestive of the power of this superstition that through many changes of tenancy and furniture the skull still holds its accustomed place "unmoved and unremoved"!

In 1903, whilst serving as Chief Justice of the Leeward Islands (in the West Indies), Udal researched the Pinney family. On Nevis he found a memorial to John Pinney, born in 1686, the son of Azariah Pinney, who has his memorial at Bettiscombe.

Azariah Pinney joined Monmouth's rebellion in 1685 and was sentenced by Judge Jeffreys to be hung drawn and quartered. He was reprieved on payment of £65 (Jeffreys was known for greed) and transported to the West Indies as a slave. Later he gained his freedom and prospered. His descendant, John Pretor Pinney, sold the family estates on Nevis and is thought to have returned to England accompanied by his faithful old black servant named Bettiscombe.

Legend has it the skull is Bettiscombe's and that his dying wish was to be buried on Nevis. His master refused to pay for this and the man Bettiscombe was buried in St Stephen's, Bettiscombe. It is said that ill fortune plagued the village afterwards and screams were heard from the burial ground. As a result, the body was exhumed and taken to the manor house, where the skull remained.

Forensic researches in 1963 confirmed Udal's surmise that the skull was that of a European woman, not a man of African heritage. Moreover, she was young, between 25 and 30 at death. More is not known, but it has been speculated that she was a fugitive or a hostage hidden at Bettiscombe Manor, or that the skull was found in one of the many local prehistoric burial sites and kept as a memento mori (a reminder of mortality).

Udal dismissed stories which grew around the legend "both in volume and romance", especially its reputation of being a "Screaming Skull". He wrote he "almost regretted" having drawn attention to the Bettiscombe skull. Nonetheless, he was evidently intrigued, as his extensive researches over the years in Bettiscombe and later on Nevis show.

Bettiscombe Manor.

Eggardon Hill - *Iron Age mysteries*
Distance: 6¾ miles/10.6km Time: 3½ hours Grade: Challenging
With short cut- Distance: 5 miles/8km Time: 2 ½ hours Grade: Moderate

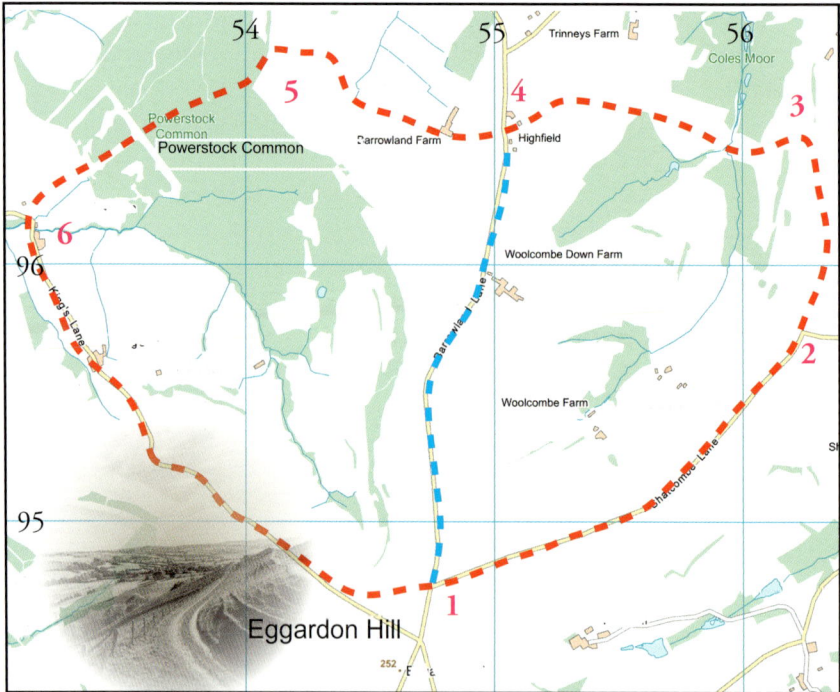

Start/parking: Park carefully at or near the Shatcombe Lane picnic area on a minor road, signed "Wynford Eagle Maiden Newton", SY54794 94773, DT6 3TF.

Terrain: Footpaths, bridleways and quiet lanes. Three ascents, two moderate, one steep (one moderate ascent only with short cut). Fairly well signed, but attention needed to map and directions.

Refreshments: Spyway Inn, Askerswell, 01308 485250.

Stiles: 6

Public Toilets: None.

Maps: Ordnance Survey OS Explorer 117 and Landranger 194.

1.   **Start SY54794 94773:** Take the lane signed "Wynford Eagle and Maiden Newton" east. Walk past the turnings for Woolcombe and Brooms Farms.

2.   **1¼ miles/1.9km SY56245 95755:** Leave the lane when it bends sharp right. Continue ahead "Private Track Bridleway Only".

3.   **1¾ miles/2.8km SY56215 96569:** Turn left at a crosstracks (marked by blue arrows). Take the right hand gate in front of you. Walk down to the bottom left field edge. Exit via a stile into a track through the trees. On your right is a pool edged by wild iris. The path divides. Keep right on the footpath as signed on a gatepost. Ignore the footpath right 200m ahead. Continue uphill on a clear path and on through fields in the same direction to a small metal gate and a stile. Turn left and follow the stony path behind the house to a lane.

4.   **2¾ miles/4.4km SY55045 96514:** You may short cut from here by turning left to the start and then turning right opposite Point 1 to follow the footpath to Eggardon. This reduces the walk by 1¾ miles/2.6km and cuts out the steep ascent from Whetley to Eggardon. For the full route cross the lane. Go through the small gate and walk down to Barrowland Farm. Dogleg left around the farm buildings. Follow the track downhill (ie the track west not the track south) and then up to a metal gate in the trees.

5.   **3½ miles/5.6km SY54095 96895:** Turn left and follow the path through Powerstock Nature Reserve and on in the same direction over rough grass to a line of trees. Turn left and then right at the bridleway gate. Follow the path ahead to Whetley.

6.   **4½ miles/7km SY53078 96207:** Turn left and follow the lane uphill for 1½ miles/2.3km. Turn right at a bridleway sign and gate to explore Eggardon. Retrace your steps to the lane and follow the permissive path over the stile to the start.

The ramparts at Eggardon Hill.

The highlight of this exploration of West Dorset's rolling hills is Eggardon (252m/831ft). An Iron Age fort and a superb viewpoint, it covers 8ha (20 acres) and is defended by three massive ramparts. The full route also includes Powerstock Common, a Nature Reserve noted for its wildflowers, butterflies and birds.

Eggardon gives a sense of tranquil timelessness...and yet is said to be haunted. Diana, goddess of the moon and hunting joins here with demons, witches and fairies collecting the souls of the dead. Dogs and horses are reported terrified on visiting Eggardon for no apparent reason, while passing motorists have had their car engines suddenly die and their watches stop.

No doubt Eggardon's supernatural reputation was very advantageous to Isaac Gulliver (1745-1822), Dorset's most successful smuggler. Eggardon was on the extensive network of inland routes along which Gulliver traded. Close to his North Eggardon Farm, it provided an excellent look out point and, with the pine trees Gulliver planted there, a daymark for his vessels bringing contraband to nearby beaches and coves. Later, the authorities realised what purpose the pines served and felled them.

Above: The ramparts on the south side of Eggardon Hill.

Sandford Orcas - *ghosts galore?*
Distance: 5½ miles/8.6km or 3¼ miles/5km Time: 3 hours or 1¾ hours
Grade: Moderate/Easy

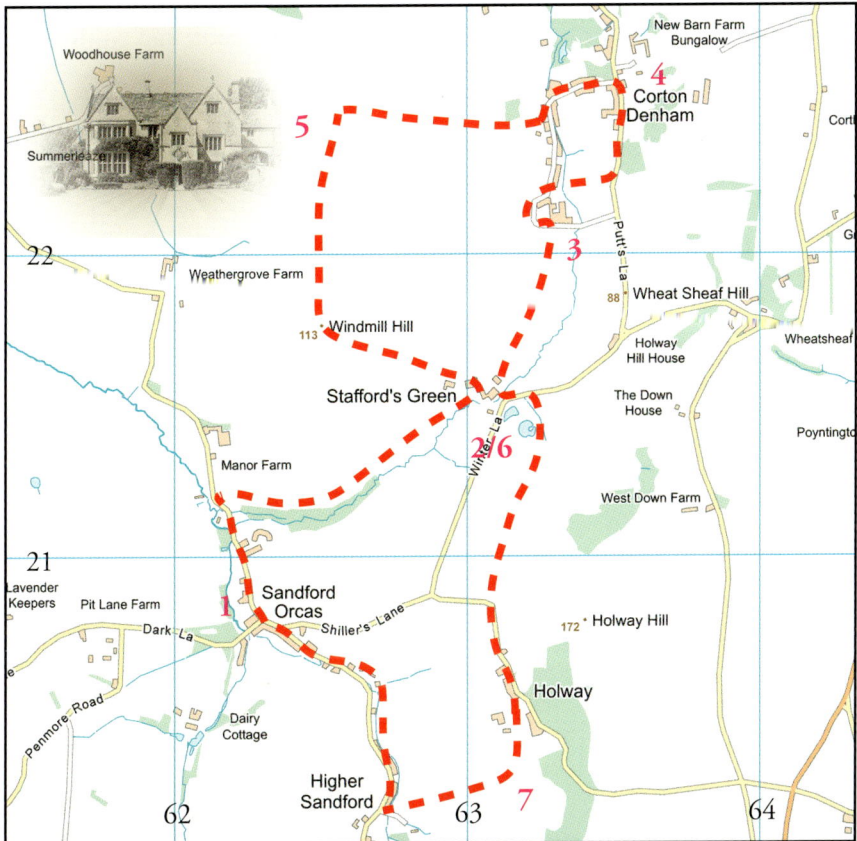

Sandford Orcas Manor opening times: 01963 220206.
Start/parking: Park with care by village hall, ST62389 20780, DT9 4RX.
Terrain: Signed field paths and quiet lanes. Fairly level: one long but gentle ascent.
Refreshments: Mitre Inn, Sandford Orcas; Queen's Arms, Corton Denham
Stiles:13
Public Toilets: None.
Maps: OS Explorer 129 (east sheet) and Landranger 183.

1.   **Start ST 62389 20780:** With the village hall on your left, head north up the main street for 200m. Divert right to visit Sandford Orcas Manor. Return to the lane and continue for 200m. Turn right across a stile. Continue in

the same direction over stiles and through fields. Cross a footbridge. Continue past farm buildings to a lane.

2.   **1¼ miles/1.9km ST63122 21542:** You may short cut from this point by following the directions from Point 6. For the full route, cross the lane and stile and follow the clear path north across a field, over a stile and on towards a farm.

3.   **1½ miles/2.5km ST63297 22096:** Reaching a lane, turn left and follow it around a dogleg. Walk ahead through a small metal gate and over two stiles. Continue straight uphill to a lane. Turn left, continue past the Queen's Arms.

4.   **2¼ miles/3.4km ST63568 22575:** Turn left into Middle Ridge Lane (or divert right to visit the church). Just after the lane turns left, turn right and uphill, signed "Woodhouse". Follow the stony track past a cemetery and uphill over a series of fields and stiles in the same direction.

5.   **2¾ miles/4.2km ST62545 22358:** At the top of the ridge, go through a small gate and turn left. Turn left at a tracks junction. Continue to point 2/6.

6.   **3½ miles/5.5km ST63122 21542:** Follow the lane as it curves left (east) for 200m. Cross a stile on the right. Continue over the fields ahead by a series of stiles and gates to a lane. Follow the lane ahead for 350m. Leave the lane and follow the bridleway ahead for 250m.

7.   **4½ miles/7.2km ST63143 20302:** Turn right at a broad metal gate as signed. Cross the field ahead to another gate. Continue to a lane. Turn right for 200m. Divert right as signed onto the footpath by a house. Follow it behind gardens and along a field edge. Turn left at a metal gate to the Mitre Inn. Turn right along the lane to the start.

The view north from point 2.

Sandford Orcas Manor.

This pleasant figure of eight route is centred on two pretty Ham Stone villages and offers splendid panoramas of the Dorset/Somerset borders; the Mendips and the Levels from Corton Ridge. Sandford Orcas Manor House dates from the 1550s. Open to the public (see below), it has many attractive features and is also reputed to be one of England's most haunted houses, with no fewer than fourteen resident ghosts.

The house's reputation for such extraordinary supernatural activity dates to the tenancy of Colonel Francis Claridge, who lived at the manor from 1964 to 1978 and opened it to visitors. Claridge regaled the press and anyone who would listen with increasingly macabre stories of the manor's history and phantoms. The phenomena include the ghost of a farmer who hanged himself in the house; a wicked priest who bends over the beds of guests and appears to be about to smother them and a sinister man who walks from the gatehouse to the staff quarters amidst the stench of decaying flesh.

Many books and websites include accounts of these phenonema. Significantly, there is no mention of the manor in J.S. Udal's definitive book *Dorsetshire Folklore* (published in 1922), although Udal details many other Dorset ghost stories.

Opinion on their veracity is, not surprisingly, divided. The present owner, Sir Mervyn Medlycott, is sceptical and considers the sudden proliferation of ghostly sightings by the Colonel were suspiciously coincidental and convenient. Sir Mervyn was quoted in a Dorset Life article (February 2015): "I can only assume the ghosts left with the tenant."

King's Stag and Lydlinch - *the phantom white hart*

Distance: 5¼ miles/8.3km Time: 2¾ hours Grade: Moderate

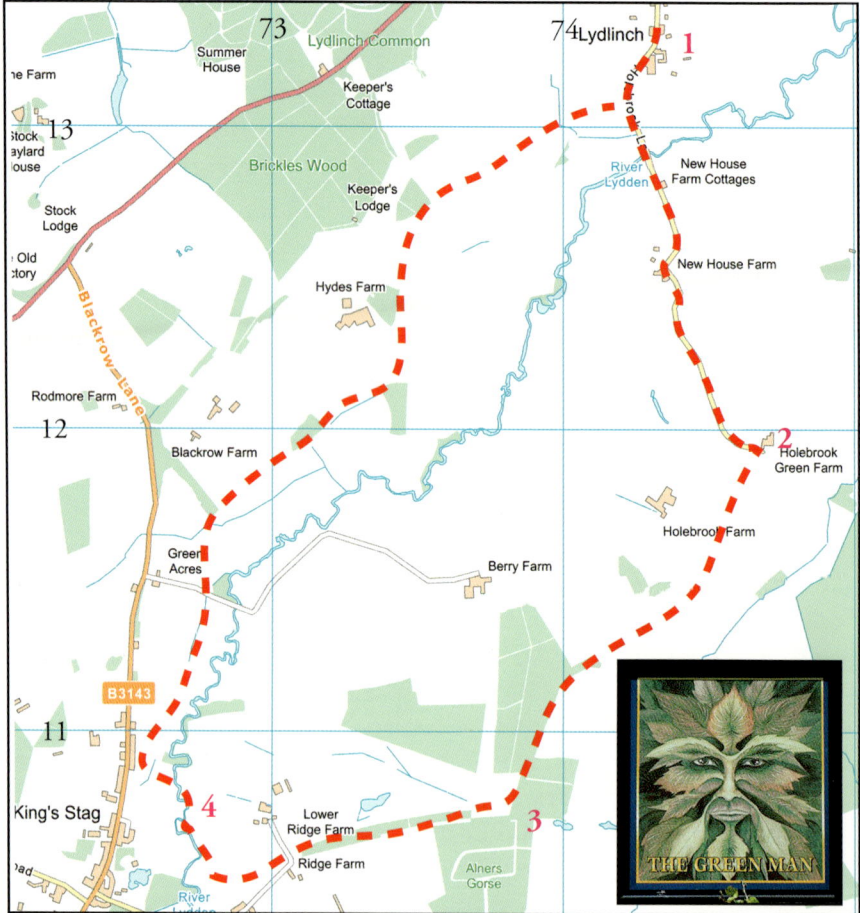

Start/parking: Park with care by Lydlinch Church, Holebrook Lane ST74319 13367, DT10 2JA.

Terrain: Largely level. Field paths, bridleways and quiet lanes. Careful attention needed to map and directions. Signing intermittent.

Refreshments: The Green Man, King's Stag, 01258 920022.

Stiles: 5   Public Toilets: None. **Maps:** Maps OS Explorer 129 (East Sheet) and Landranger 194.

1.   **Start ST74319 13367:** Follow Holebrook Lane south to Holebrook Green Farm.

2.	**1 mile/1.7km ST74690 11931:** Ignore the grassy vehicle track facing you at the end of the main track. Turn right opposite the farm through a gate and walk ahead with the field edge on your right. Continue through a pair of small gates. Cut straight across the large field ahead. Exit through a small metal gate. Follow the woodland path ahead.

3.	**2 miles/3.2km ST73833 10722:** Reaching a crosstrack (Ridge Drove) turn right. (NB do not follow the path into Almer's Gorse Copse). At a farm track keep left as signed and turn almost immediately right over a pair of stiles and follow the well-beaten grassy path ahead, diverging away from the track. Stay on the path when it turns right. Keep the hedge on your left. Follow the path left through a gateway. Continue ahead with the hedge on your right and on over a small footbridge. Follow the path right to a second footbridge.

4.	**3 miles/4.8km ST72615 10909**: Cross the bridge and follow the field path ahead along the right field edge. At the top of the field turn left then right through a signed gateway. Continue ahead. Cross a tarred track. Walk across the next field to a gate. Continue along the left field edge as signed to join a track. When the track forks keep right to avoid Hydes Farm. Near the top of the slope and before reaching the farm itself, turn right through a gate. Walk ahead with the field edge on your left through a gate and up to a broad farm track. Turn right. Ignore the stile 100m ahead. Take the second of two tracks on the right. This leads to a bridge. Cross and turn immediately right through a gate. Cut diagonally right across this field to a gate. Follow the next field edge. Bear right and cut diagonally right across a large field to meet a lane. Turn left to the start.

Below left: Lydlinch Church and right: The village sign at King's Stag.

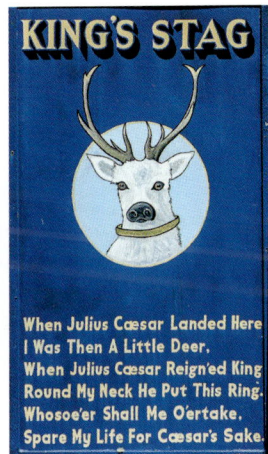

This gentle walk through the rich green pastures of the Blackmore Vale, so well described in Thomas Hardy's novel *Tess of the D'Urbervilles*, centres on the legend of a white hart. King Henry III (reigned 1207-1272) was particularly fond of hunting in Blackmore Vale. After a long and strenuous chase, Henry ran his quarry to bay and found it to be a beautiful white hart. Henry let it go unharmed: a kingly gesture: white deer are exceedingly rare, which may explain why they symbolise royalty.

Sometime later, a local gentleman, Sir Thomas de la Linde, hunted and killed the white hart, though he knew of King Henry's encounter with it. Furious, Henry threw de la Linde into prison, fining him heavily. From that time forth de la Linde's estate was obliged to pay a yearly tax of "White Hart Silver" to the Crown.

The white hart was said to have lived for centuries in Blackmore's wooded vale. When de la Linde slew it, a golden collar was found around its neck. Inscribed upon it were ancient words, which today grace the sign which stands on a small green in King's Stag. (Photo)

Lulworth and Durdle Door - *dancers on the waves*

Distance: 4¾ miles/7.4km Time: 2½ hours Grade: Moderate

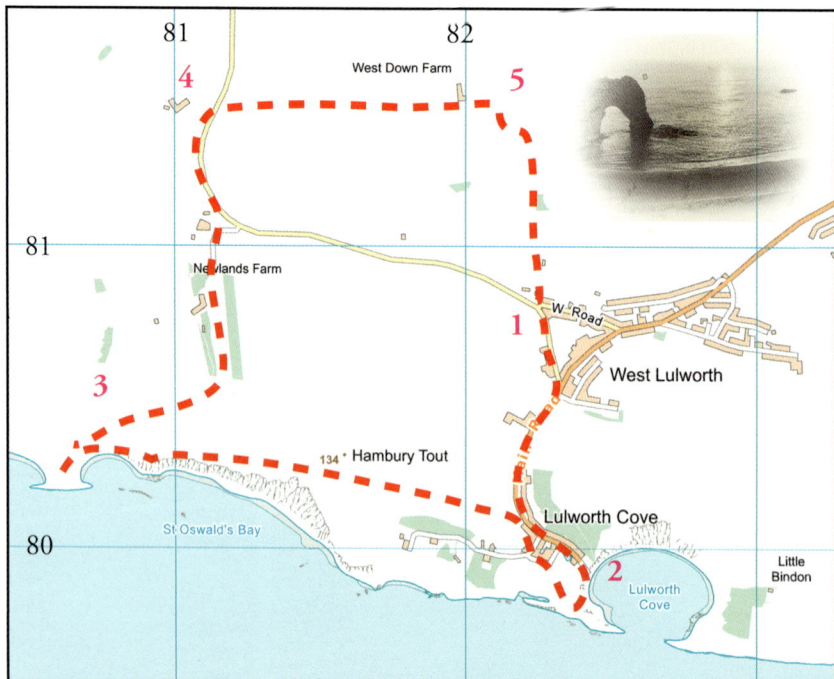

Start/parking: Roadside parking with care by Lulworth church SY82267 80799, BH20 5RY. (Alternatively, use the large car park at Point 2).
Terrain: Coastpath, footpaths, quiet lanes. Two steep ascents and descents.
Refreshments: Choice of cafés, pubs and restaurants in West Lulworth.
Stiles: 1
Public Toilets: Lulworth Cove.
Maps: Ordnance Survey OL15 and Landranger 194.

1.   **Start SY82267 80799:** Follow the lane downhill to a fork. Cross the lane and turn right into the footpath. Continue to the Heritage Centre (well worth visiting).

?   **½ mile/0.8km SY82227 80077:** Continue ahead to the beach. Turn sharp right up steps, signed "Coastpath". Follow the path right around Stair Hole. Bear right to return to Point 2. Follow the signed Coastpath across the car park and uphill via steps. Follow the Coastpath down to a fingerpost.

3.   **1¾ miles/2.9km SY81062 80458:** At the time of writing (June 2020), walkers were obliged to follow a one way loop to Durdle Door. Instead of turning left (as previously) signed "Durdle Door", continue ahead as directed to a path fork. Bear left and left at two more path turns for Durdle Door. Return to Point 3 as directed. (It is not known whether this diversion will be temporary). From Point 3, continue ahead through the car park and along the access lane. Reaching the road, turn left along the verge for 400m to Dagger's Gate.

4.   **3½ miles/5.6km SY81104 81394:** Turn right, signed "West Down The Drove" along a broad track.

5.   **4¼ miles/6.6km SY82064 81522:** Turn right at a waymark just past

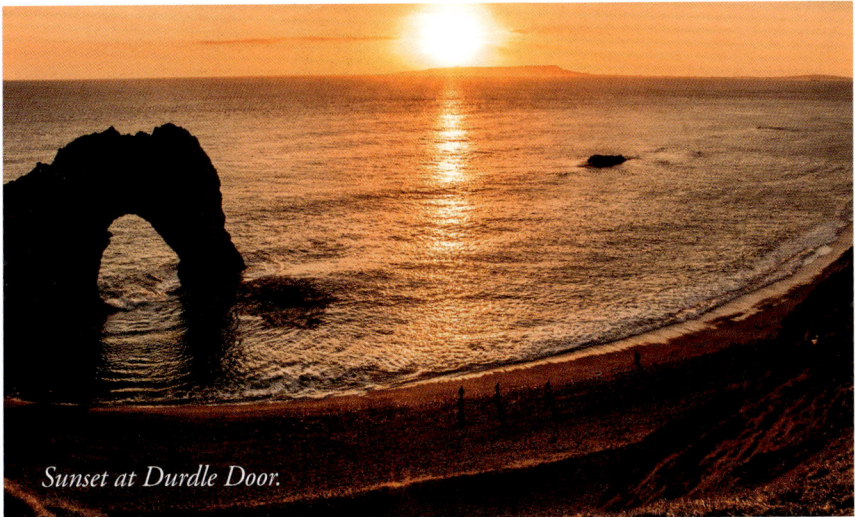

Sunset at Durdle Door.

West Down Farm. Keep the field edge on your left. Continue downhill through fields, keeping the hedge on your left to a tarmac drive. Continue ahead to the start.

This fairly demanding but very rewarding walk includes some of the finest scenery and rock formations on Dorset's Jurassic Coast. The almost perfect circle of Lulworth Cove was formed by an ancient river breaching the hard Purbeck and Portland limestones, allowing the sea to scour away the softer Wealden sediments behind. Durdle Door is composed of the same hard limestones. Its impressive arch was formed by the sea, which exploited and ate through a weakness in the protruding rock. Marine erosion also formed the arches and coves at Stair Hole, whilst the Purbeck Beds there were crumpled by tectonic forces.

Durdle Door and Lulworth Cove are said to be haunted. Purbeck was strongly defended during WW2, whilst Lulworth Cove was sealed off and mined, with lookouts posted along the cliffs. Happily, the much feared enemy invasion never materialised, but the lookouts were astonished to see dancers in the moonlight on Lulworth's beach – strictly against orders. Suddenly, they vanished. The area was carefully searched and the defences checked, but the ghostly dancers reappeared some nights later, while at Durdle Door, apparitions of young girls were reported dancing on the waves.

Looking back towards Lulworth Cove.

Tolpuddle and Athelhampton House - *a ghostly ape*

Distance: 5½ miles/8.7km Time: 3 hours Grade: Moderate

Start/parking: Roadside parking by Tolpuddle Martyrs' Museum SY78829 94522, DT2 7EH.
Terrain: Bridlepaths and quiet lanes. Mainly level. No steep slopes.
Refreshments: Martyrs Inn, Tolpuddle 01305 848249.
Stiles: 0
Public Toilets: None.
Athelhampton House: Check opening times 01305 848363.
Tolpuddle Martyrs Museum: 01305 848237.
Maps: OS Explorer OL15 (east sheet) and Landranger 194.

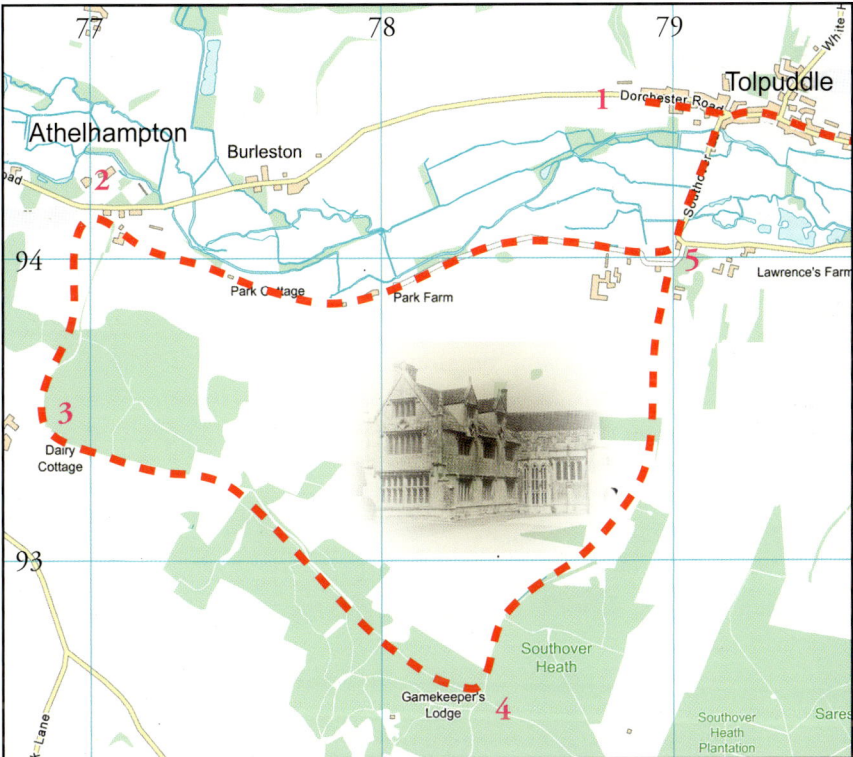

1.   **Start SY78829 94522:** Turn left along the village street. Turn right at The Green by the Martyrs' Tree and Memorial Shelter. Follow the lane ahead. When it bends sharp left, continue straight ahead, then immediately right through a gate. Follow the bridleway into an enclosed path and on along a

The bridleway to Athelhampton

broad farm track. Continue through Park Farm as signed and along the field edge ahead past a thatched cottage and into a track.

2.　　　**1¾ miles/2.9km SY77083 94144:** Reaching a bridleway junction divert right to visit Athelhampton House. Cross the road carefully and turn left along the verge. Turn right into the drive. Return to Point 2. Walk ahead and uphill along an enclosed path. When the path forks keep ahead (right) through trees to a path junction. (NB the path is not exactly as shown on the Explorer map: it skirts Admiston Farm and the adjoining field to the east of it and stays within the woodland).

3.　　　**2¼ miles/3.7km SY76973 93382:** Turn left. Follow the path along the woodland edge. Continue ahead through a metal gate and follow the upper field edge. Follow the path into woodland.

4.　　　**3¼ miles/5.2km SY78364 92544:** Reaching a crosstracks, turn left. Follow the stony track ahead, ignoring side turnings. Continue to a lane.

5.　　　**4¼ miles/6.9km SY79033 94055:** Turn left. Follow the lane as it bends sharp right. Retrace your steps to the Martyrs' Tree. Consult the map on the plaque. Turn right to visit the Martyrs' Inn; Martyrs' Cottage; the Old Chapel and the Methodist Chapel with its memorial arch. From there, retrace your steps to the start.

This gentle field and woodland walk includes one of England's most haunted houses and a village with a proud place in British labour history. National attention was focussed on Tolpuddle in 1834 when six local farm labourers were sentenced to transportation, nominally for swearing an illegal oath, in reality for forming a trade union and thus challenging the authority of landowners and magistrates, the rural Establishment. Their savage sentences of seven years caused a national outcry. After a three year long campaign the men were "pardoned" by King William IV. Their dramatic story and the harsh realities of 19th century life in rural Dorset are told in the Tolpuddle Martyrs Museum and the "Tolpuddle Martyrs Trail" around the village.

Athelhampton House

Athelhampton dates from the 15th century. Visitors first enter the Great Hall, where a guest was disturbed by the apparitions of two young men In 17th century garb fighting a duel. She demanded they stop, but they ignored her and fought on until one was injured, At this point, they left the room. When the lady asked the owner who they might be, he was as perplexed as she.

A pet ape haunts the priest hole. The unfortunate animal was accidentally imprisoned and died of thirst in this secret passage, built to hide Catholic clergy during religious persecutions. Though never seen, its ghostly scratching can be heard as it tries desperately to escape.

The Great Stairway is haunted by a cat: the soft padding of its paws has been reported several times. One of the housemaids saw the figure of a priest by the bathroom, whilst the sound of tapping from the wine cellar is ascribed to a ghostly cooper. Visitors to the King's Room have reported feeling inexplicably cold and uncomfortable, phenomena often associated with ghosts. Haunted too is the State Bedroom: a grey lady sits on the bed, but she will disappear if asked to do so.

Right: The wonderful fifteenth century west front of Athelhampton House.

Clouds Hill and T.E. Lawrence - *his ghostly motorcycle*

Distance: 5 miles/8.1km Time: 2½ hours Grade: Moderate

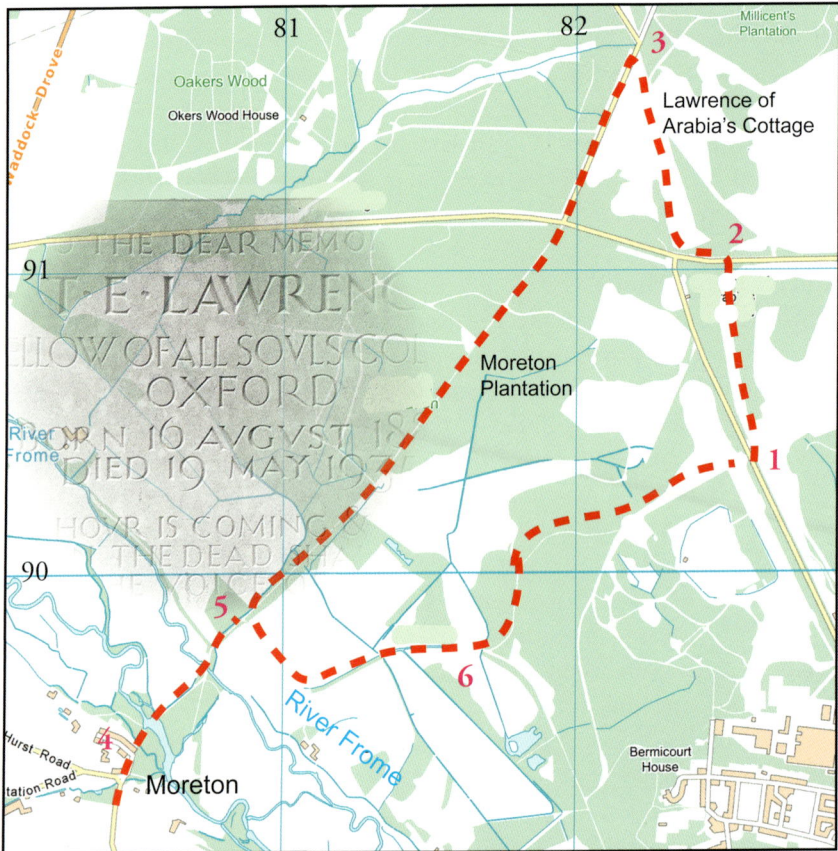

Start/parking: Parking area 500m south Cloud's Hill by Lawrence's Memorial Stone, SY82595 90425, BH20 7NQ.

Terrain: Mainly level, no steep slopes. Signed tracks and lanes.

Refreshments: Dovecote Café in the Walled Garden.

Stiles: 0

Public Toilets: None.

Maps: OS Explorer OL15 or Landranger 194.

Cloud's Hill (National Trust) 01929 405616, www.nationaltrust.org.uk

1.   **Start SY82595 90425:** Take the signed path by Lawrence's memorial stone "Lawrence Trail Clouds Hill". Continue past a second memorial stone.

2.   **¼ mile/0.5km SY82536 91025:** Reaching the road, turn left "Lawrence Trail Clouds Hill Moreton". Follow the verge to the T junction for Clouds Hill. To avoid the busy road ahead, cross carefully and follow the signed bridleway opposite. Go through the gate and follow the clear path north-west over the heath.

3.   **1 mile/1.5km SY82213 91736:** Reaching a lane, turn left, signed "Moreton Bovington Camp". Cross the road carefully. Walk ahead on a stony track, "Lawrence Trail Moreton". Reaching a crosstracks, continue ahead "Moreton". This leads over a bridge into the village.

4.   **2¾ miles/4.3km SY80482 89410:** Walk ahead for 100m to the cemetery. Lawrence's grave is on the right at the back by a wooden cross. Exit; turn left to view the Walled Garden, five acres of plants and flowers with the Dovecote Café. Retrace your steps past the cemetery. Turn first right to visit the church and its remarkable engraved windows by Laurence Whistler. Retrace your steps over the bridge. Continue to a signed track on the right, "Lawrence Trail, Bovington".

5.   **3¾ miles/5.9km SY80862 89856:** Follow this track to a fork.

6.   **4¼ miles/6.8km SY81710 89751:** Bear left "Lawrence Trail Clouds Hill". Keep right at the next fork (the sign was damaged at the time of writing). The flinty track climbs steadily to a gate. It then continues through trees and between fences to the start.

Previous page: The track near Cloud's Hill. Below: A window in Moreton Church.

Following the Lawrence Trail, this route explores woodland and heath and passes by Clouds Hill (National Trust), the retreat of T.E. Lawrence, the legendary and enigmatic "Lawrence of Arabia". His strong, complex and often contradictory personality is deeply impressed upon this tiny labourer's cottage, which he restored, altered and furnished.

After completing his RAF service in 1935, Lawrence retired to Clouds Hill, looking much younger and fitter than his 46 years. His magnum opus, *Seven Pillars of Wisdom*, had sold extraordinarily well and his future appeared to offer rich new possibilities for his undoubted talents. They were not to be fulfilled. Only a few weeks later, he died from his injuries after losing control of his Brough Superior motorcycle near Clouds Hill after swerving to avoid collision with two young cyclists. The roar of Lawrence's Brough is said to haunt the road before dawn.

His funeral drew many notable mourners, among them Winston and Clementine Churchill, who had known Lawrence well. The funeral also drew the national press and, perhaps inevitably, a series of conspiracy theories about his sudden death arose which persist today.

Lawrence's untimely death was re-examined and developed by filmmaker Mark Griffin in *Lawrence After Arabia* in 2020 . Griffin postulates the British Secret Services were responsible for Lawrence's sudden death and that a D-notice was put on the case to stifle media enquiry. Central to this scenario is a mysterious black car that was never identified. It was reported by Corporal Catchpole, one of the witnesses at the inquest (which found Lawrence's death an accident). Catchpole stated that just before Lawrence swerved, he passed a black car driving in the opposite direction. However, a plaque near the scene of Lawrence's death states neither of the cyclists recalled the car and indeed swore there was no car.

According to Griffin, Churchill had Lawrence earmarked as future head of the Secret Service, which caused intense resentment in that quarter, as did Lawrence's continuing links with leading Arabs. Griffin avers the supposed black car collided with Lawrence's motorcycle, causing him to swerve and inflicting marked damage on the machine. However, the filmmaker did not reach a firm conclusion on whether TE Lawrence was assassinated or died accidentally.

At this distance in time it seems unlikely the possibility of assassination will ever be firmly established – or conclusively and finally debunked. More than a century after the First World War and nearly sixty years after David Lean's coup de cinema, *Lawrence of Arabia*, interest in T.E. Lawrence remains as strong as ever.

Winterborne Zelston - *the Red Post*

Distance: 7¼ miles/11.5km Time: 3½ hours Grade: Moderate

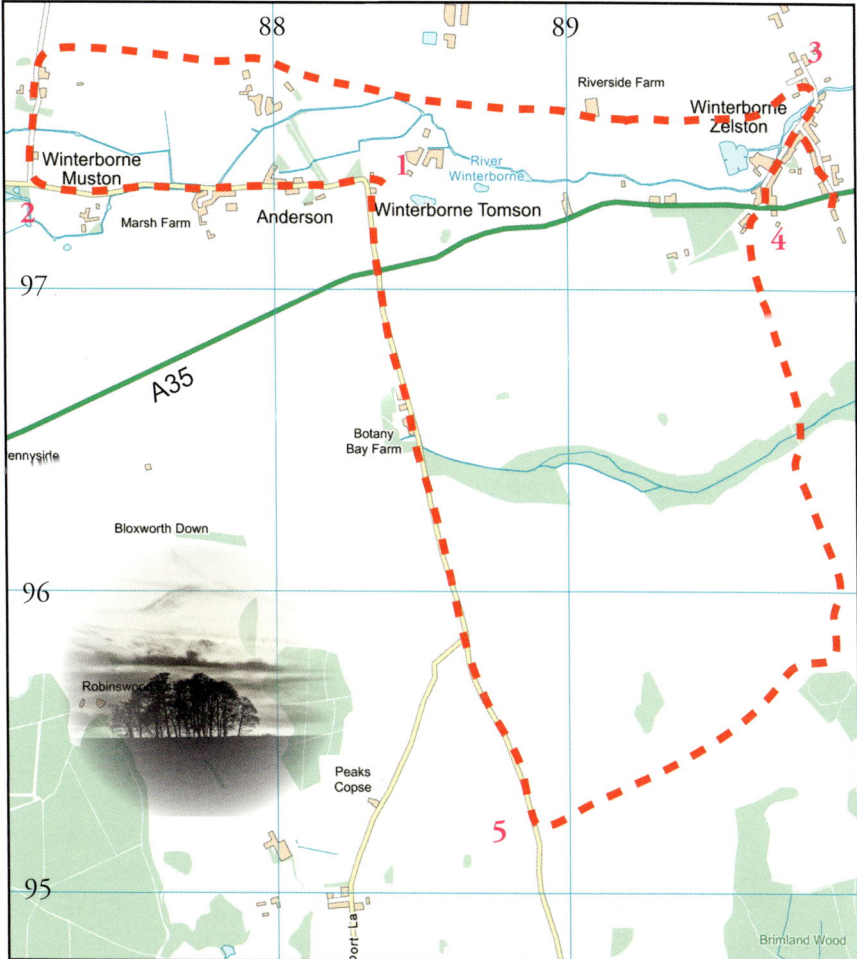

Start/parking: St Andrew's church, Winterborne Tomson, SY885 974 , DT11 9HA.

Terrain: Field paths, tracks and lanes. No steep slopes. Parts muddy. Signage variable in quality. Attention to map and directions needed.

Stiles: 0

Refreshments: Botany Bay Inn, 01929 459227.

Public Toilets: None.

Maps: Ordnance Survey Explorer 118; Landranger 194 and 195.

1.   **Start SY885 974:** After visiting the church, walk down the lane towards A31. Turn first right at the lane junction.

2.   **1mile/1.6km SY872 974:** Take the second lane right. Turn right between farm buildings, opposite the farmhouse. Follow a tarred track. Turn left through a kissing gate. Follow the path east across fields, passing just north farm of buildings. Continue east along field edges as signed, then along a tarred track. Walk between farm buildings. Turn right and almost immediately left. Continue as signed along field edges.

3.   **3 miles/4.8km SY898 977:** Turn right into the village. Walk past the church. Divert first left to visit the Botany Bay Inn. Retrace your steps to the lane junction. Turn left to the A31.

4.   **3¾ miles/6km SY897 973:** Cross the road carefully. Follow the bridleway ahead for only 100m. Turn left onto a signed bridleway, an enclosed track with two dogleg turns. Cross a footbridge. Follow the track right into field. Turn left. Follow the track along the left field edge to a wood. Turn right as signed.

5.   **5¾ miles/9.1km SY889 953:** Turn right onto a tarred lane. Continue past Botany Bay Farm to the A31. Cross carefully. Turn first right "Historic Church". Continue to the start.

Enjoy this pleasant, gentle route through the Dorset fields and lanes, starting from Winterborne Tomson's beautiful Norman church, with its box pews and two decker pulpit. En route we visit the Botany Bay Inn, pass Botany Bay Farm and a curious red signpost, pointing the way to an overnight stop for prisoners marching in chains from Dorchester Prison to Portsmouth and thence the long voyage to the Botany Bay penal settlements in Australia. Botany Bay Farm was a stopping place for the convicts, among them the Tolpuddle Martyrs (page 27). Originally the General Allenby, the Botany Bay Inn changed its name to mark the Australian bicentenary in 1988.

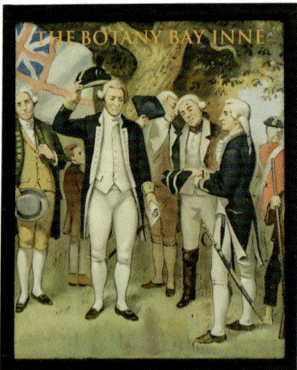

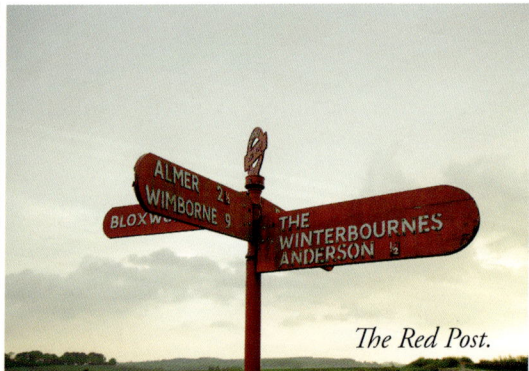

The Red Post.

Badbury Rings - *ghostly warriors*

Distance: 4¼ miles/6.7km Time: 2 hours Grade: Easy

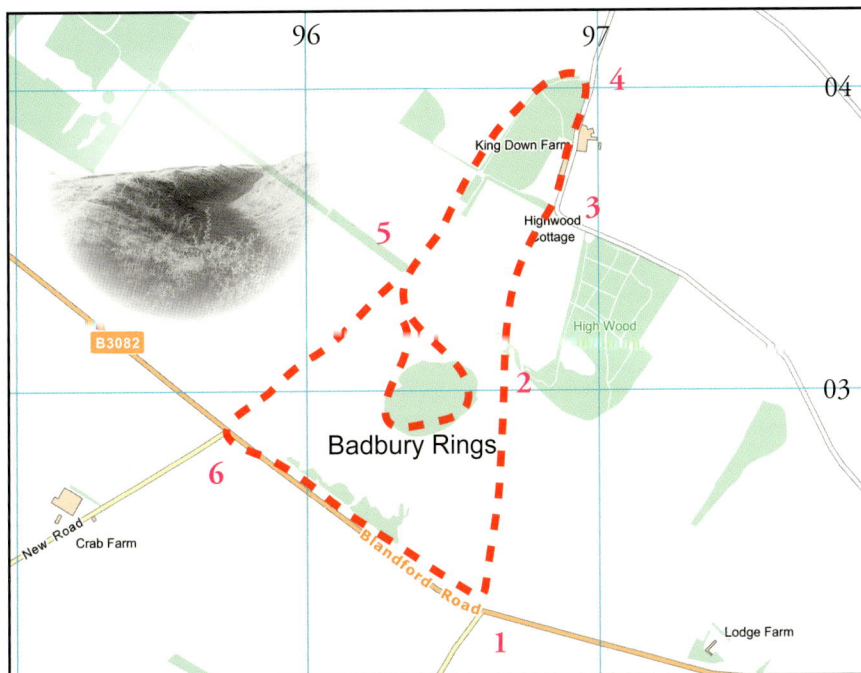

Start/parking: Parking area on the Wimborne/Blandford road opposite turning for Sturminster Marshall, ST96628 02295, BH21 4DZ.
Terrain: Mainly level or gently undulating. Clear tracks and paths.
Refreshments: True Lover's Knot, Tarrant Keyneston 01258 452209.
Stiles: 1
Public Toilets: None.
Maps: OS Explorer 118 and Landranger 195.

1. **Start ST96628 02295:** With your back to the road, take the path ahead (north-west).
2. **½ mile/0.8km ST96724 03072:** You may short cut at this point by turning left through the metal gate onto Badbury Rings and following the directions from * in Point 5. For the full route, walk ahead.
3. **1 mile/1.4km ST96848 03612:** Continue ahead "Witchampton" on reaching a path junction at the Oaks.
4. **1¼ miles/1.9km ST96983 04033:** Take the next turning left. Walk ahead. Take the metal gate on the right and turn left, following the track along

the woodland edge. At a crosstracks continue ahead in the same direction (south-west) on the broad path.

5.	**1¾ miles/2.8km ST96321 03384:** Turn left at the waymark, just before a gate. Cross the stile and circuit Badbury Rings by turning left and then bearing right over the turf to follow one of the three rampart paths. Each gives a different, but vivid perspective. At intervals there are steps. Divert to the centre of the fort to see the viewing table. *Having completed your circuit of Badbury Rings, return to Point 5. Turn left and walk ahead with the fence on your right. Continue through the car park, down the stony track to meet a grassy path running parallel to the beech avenue.

6.	**3½ miles/5.7km ST95770 02971:** Turn left along the path and follow it to the start.

Badbury Rings is an Iron Age hillfort. Standing 100m (327ft) above sea level, it offers sweeping views across a wide expanse of country. It can be freely explored and a circuit of its rampart gives a vivid idea of its considerable size and defensive potential.

The hillfort was constructed in two phases. In the first, some 18 acres (7.3ha), were enclosed by multiple ditches. In the second, the fort was more than doubled in size to 41 acres (16.6ha) and enclosed by its still impressive ditch and ramparts. The area around the hillfort has a rich history, including earlier Bronze Age round barrows. Five Roman roads (including Ackling Dyke page 47) formed a complex junction on the north side of Badbury Rings. A mile south-west was the Romano-British town of Vindocladia.

Badbury Rings.

Badbury Rings is said to have been the site of the Battle of Badon, though Bathampton Down in Somerset and Bowden Hill in Linlithgow also claim that honour. It's generally agreed Badon was a British victory in the early 6th century which severely checked the Saxons' westward advance.

King Arthur reputedly killed at least 160 men at the Battle of Badon. He and his spectral army return from time to time to Badbury Rings. Archaeology students camping on Badbury Rings in 1970 were so terrified when awoken one night by clashing swords, marching feet and cries that they fled their tents. Similar manifestations continued for several years afterwards. A ghostly warrior with a hideously scarred face was reported, as well as another warrior on horseback, a woman in black and a menacing dwarf peering at couples.

The last section of the walk parallels a magnificent two mile long beech avenue, planted in 1835 by William John Bankes, owner of Kingston Lacy estate.

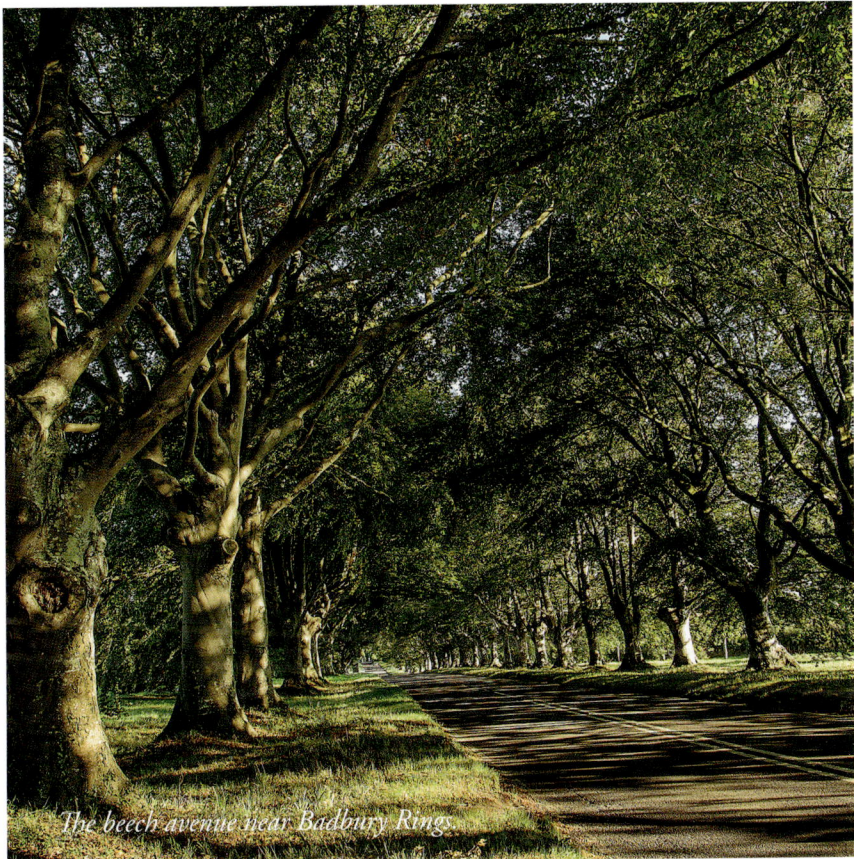

The beech avenue near Badbury Rings.

A **Studland and Godlingston Heath** - *a donkey ghost*
Distance: 5 miles/8km Time; 2½ hours Grade: Moderate
and
B **Studland to Handfast and Ballard Points** - *the smugglers' witch*
Distance: 4¾ miles/7.4km Time: 2½ hours Grade Easy/Moderate

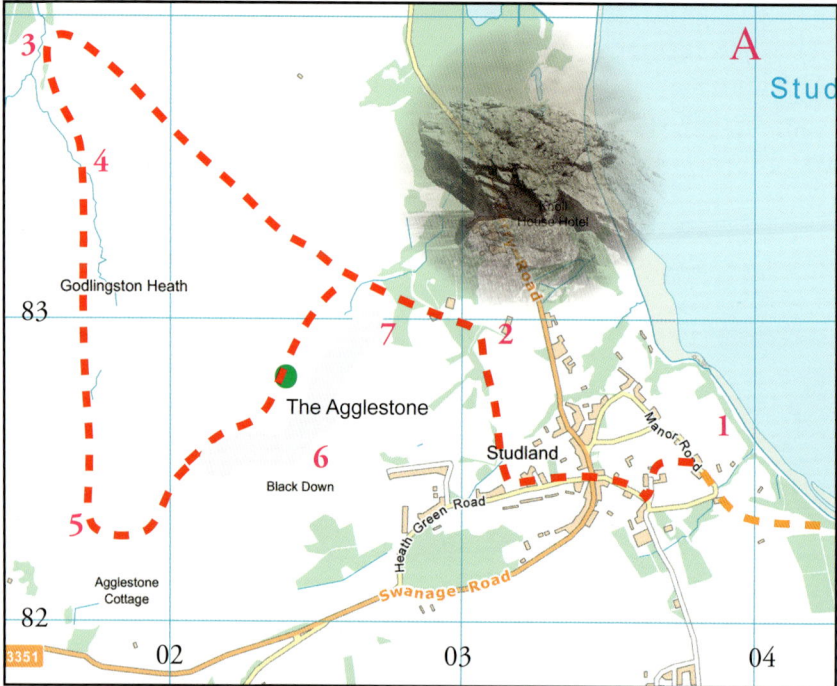

A

Start/parking: National Trust's South Sands car park Studland, SZ03717 82541, BH19 3AU.

Terrain: Tracks and paths, section of quiet lane. Some ups and downs, but no tough slopes. *Paths do not always correspond exactly with the Ordnance Survey's OL15, so careful attention to the directions is needed. Moreover, animal and vehicle tracks can come and go on the heath. A compass is very helpful.

Refreshments: Bankes Arms, Studland, 01929 450225.

Stiles: 0

Public Toilets: Studland, 200m downhill from start.

Maps: Explorer OL15 and Landranger 195.

1.   **Start SZ03717 82541:** Exit the car park from the top right corner. Walk through the churchyard. Leave by the tarred path leading up the slope from the tower. Reaching a lane, turn right. Cross over into Heath Green Road. After 200m, turn right into the bridleway, signed "Godlingston Heath". When the path forks, keep right. Follow the blue bridleway signs to a path junction. Turn right.

2.   **¾ mile/1.1km SZ03069 82988:** Turn left at a second bridleway junction. Walk past Wadmore Farm. Continue ahead. Cross a bridge. Fork right when the path divides. The Agglestone appears on the left, Studland Bay on the right. Keep right when the path forks. At the next signpost, continue ahead, signed "Greenlands", cutting diagonally left across the turf to the end of a line of gorse.

3.   **1¾ miles/2.8km SZ01572 83765:** Turn sharp left at the bridleway marker – easily missed as it is only 18 inches high. (NB this path junction is

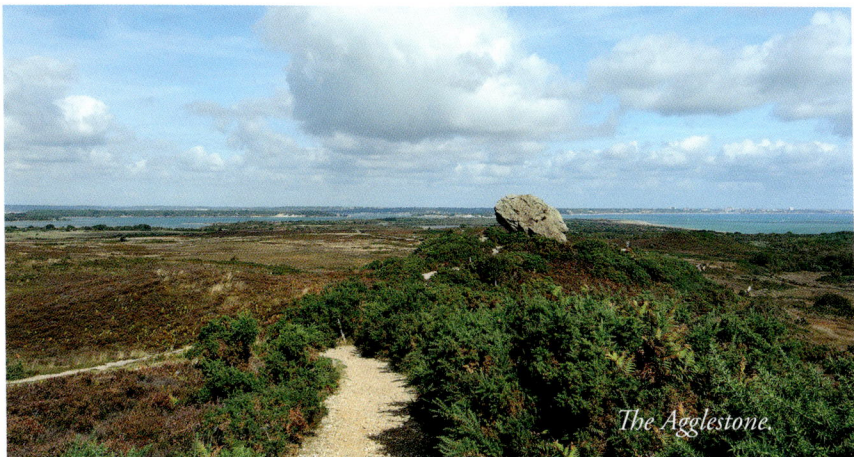

The Agglestone.

some 350m south of where it is shown on the OS Explorer map). Follow this path south.

4.   **2 miles/3.2km SZ01711 83542:** Turn right at the next path junction along a broad track. Pass just to the left of a small hill.

5.   **2¾ miles/4.3km SZ01644 82455:** Turn left at the next waymark, signed "Studland" – again the position of this path junction differs from the OS map. Turn next left onto a stony track (SZ 01926 82506). Take the next track right (SZ 02785 82815) and follow it around to the Agglestone.

6.   **3½ miles/5.5km SZ02366 82841:** Take the clear path down steps, heading north-east.

7.   **3¾ miles/6km SZ02612 83134:** Reaching a path junction, turn right and retrace your steps to the start.

This walk (which may be combined with Old Harry Rocks) explores Godlingston Heath, and offers fine views of Studland Bay, Poole Harbour and Bournemouth. Heathland once covered much of south-east Dorset. Much has been built over, turned into farmland or forest, but Godlingston retains the wildness and brooding atmosphere Thomas Hardy evoked as "Egdon Heath".

The Agglestone is perched on a knoll and a marvellous viewpoint. Composed of sandstone, 18ft high, 80ft in circumference and weighing 500 tons, it is all that is left of a thick layer of sandstone which once covered the heath, but has been eroded away over the millennia. Legend has it the Devil cast it here from the Isle of Wight. It was a poor shot - Satan was aiming for Corfe Castle.

Smugglers brought their goods over the heath on pack animals from the beaches hard by. Fortunately for them (and perhaps not coincidentally), Godlingston Heath, like Eggardon (page 14) was reputedly haunted, this time by a donkey, whose master was murdered here in the 18th century. The animal is said to have appeared to several people on the anniversary of his master's death.

A stonechat on the heath.

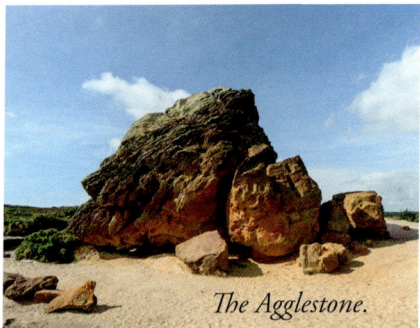

The Agglestone.

The Pinnacles

Old Harry Rocks.

B

Start/parking: National Trust car park Studland by Bankes Arms, SZ03717 82541, BH19 3AU.

Terrain: Coastpath, mainly level to Handfast Point; steady ascent to Ballard Point.

Refreshments: Bankes Arms, Studland, 01929 450225.

Stiles: 0   **Public Toilets:** Studland, 200m downhill from start.

Maps: Explorer OL15 and Landranger 195.

1.   **Start SZ03717 82541:** Turn right down the lane past the Bankes Arms. Turn left "Old Harry Rocks".

2.   **1¼ miles/2km SZ05449 82392:** Either retrace your steps from Handfast Point, or follow the Coastpath south for fine views of the Pinnacles and Swanage Bay. (Keep left of the fence).

3.   **2¼ miles/3.7km SZ04579 81314:** Retrace your steps from Ballard Point.

The highlight of this classic walk (which can be combined with Godlingston Heath, page 37) is the views over Studland and Swanage Bays, especially Old Harry Rocks. These two high vantage points were used by smugglers to signal to their colleagues at sea whether "the coast was clear".

Contraband was also taken off luggers anchored under Ballard Point and hauled up the cliff, before being taken over Ballard Down by teams of packhorses to Jenny Gould's house at nearby Ulwell. Jenny's reputation as a witch helped deter unwanted enquiries, just as ghostly stories attached to Godlingston Heath and Eggardon (page 14) discouraged snooping.

Tarrant Gunville and Eastbury House - *the ghostly steward*

Distance: 4¾ miles/7.5km Time: 2½ hours Grade: Moderate

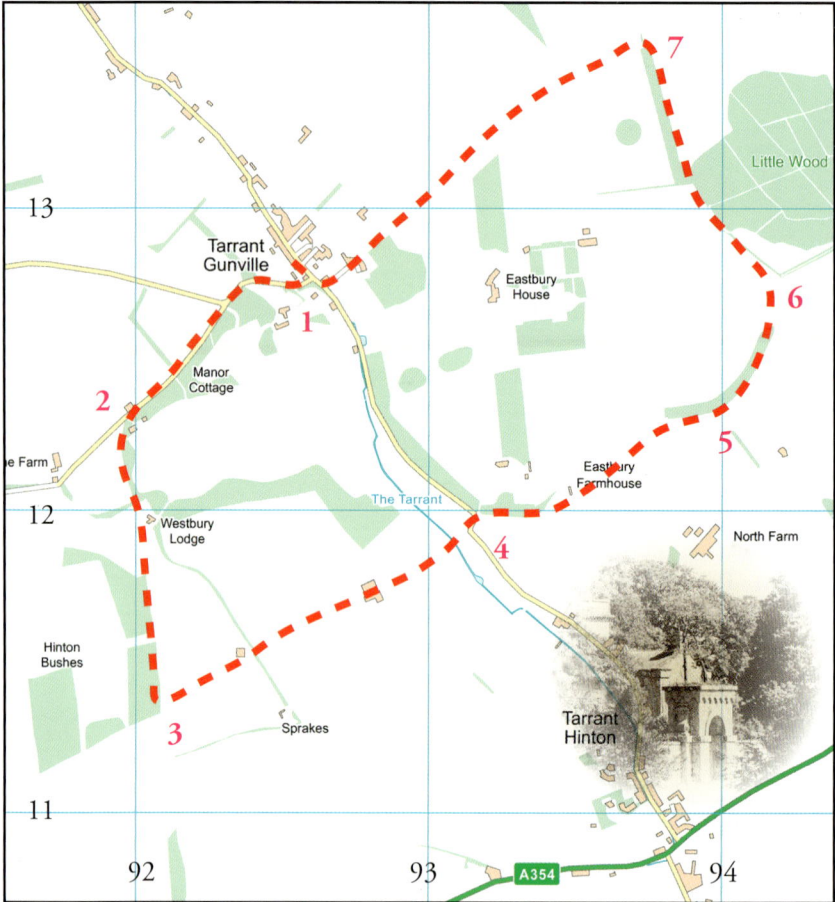

Start/parking: Park carefully on side street by the village hall, ST92561 12856, DT11 8JN.

Terrain: Clear tracks and paths, quiet lanes. Gently undulating, one short ascent.

Refreshments: Anvil Inn and Farquharson's Arms, Pimperne.

Stiles: 0 **Public Toilets:** None.

Maps: OS Explorer 118 (north sheet) and Landranger 195.

1.   **Start ST92561 12856:** With your back to the village hall, turn left down the main village street. Turn right uphill "Everley Hill Church". (Di-

vert left to visit the church). Turn left "Home Farm Only" along a well-tarred track.

2.   **¾ mile/1.3km ST91953 12291:** Turn left into a signed Public Bridleway, which begins as a stony track, later becoming a well-beaten path. Ignore side turnings.

3.   **1¼ miles/2.1km ST92094 11372:** Reaching a junction of tracks, turn left, heading north-east. Continue to a lane.

4.   **2 miles/3.3km ST93147 11958:** Walk ahead 50m and turn right into a dead end lane. On your left is Eastbury Park. Continue past a brick house on the earthen track.

5.   **2¾ miles/4.3km ST93991 12342:** Reaching a three-way junction, bear left "Byway open to all Traffic".

6   **3 miles/4.8km ST94201 12785:** Turn left onto the Public Bridleway at the next path junction.

7.   **3¾ miles/5.8km ST93729 13595:** Turn left through a small metal gate in the hedge as signed. Turn left along the field edge and right 100m ahead at the field corner. On the left at the end of this field are what look like prehistoric tumuli incorporated into the landscaping of Eastbury Park and marked on the Explorer map as "Solomon's Quarter". Continue ahead on the broad track to a small metal gate. Walk on along the enclosed path. Between the magnificent beeches are tantalising glimpses of Eastbury House. Follow the path into woodland. Turn right down a lane and 50m ahead turn right into an enclosed footpath. Follow this past a playpark. Turn left to the start.

Below left and top right: Two views of the remaining parts of once grand Eastbury House. Bottom right: Tumuli near Solomon's Quarter.

This gentle walk offers fine views over the Dorset Downs and circuits Eastbury Park, laid out and planted in classic 18th century style. Eastbury as glimpsed today from public paths (it is not open to the public) is a substantial and stately Grade 1 listed building, yet is only the magnificent stables of what was once Dorset's largest mansion.

Described as "one of the grandest and most superb in the county, indeed in the kingdom", the house proved impractically huge and expensive. In the late 18th century the 2nd Earl Temple ordered its demolition from his retreat in Italy and placed his steward, William Doggett, in charge. Doggett sold the valuable materials and pocketed the profits.

Hearing his master was making an unexpected return, Doggett panicked and shot himself in the house. It is said Doggett's blood left on the marble floor could not be cleaned, that doors would open by themselves and an apparition was seen "his face a mass of blood". When Doggett's corpse was exhumed the body was not in the least decomposed, the steward's face retaining a rosy complexion - although the course of the fatal bullet from his jaw through his head was clearly visible.

In further elaborations of the tale, a coach driven by headless horses and a headless coachman conveys Doggett's ghost to the house. Doggett proceeds to the room where he shot himself ....and shoots himself again.

The once impressive gateway to Eastbury House.

Ashmore - *"gabbygammies"*

Distance: 5½ miles/8.9km Time: 2¾ hours Grade: Moderate

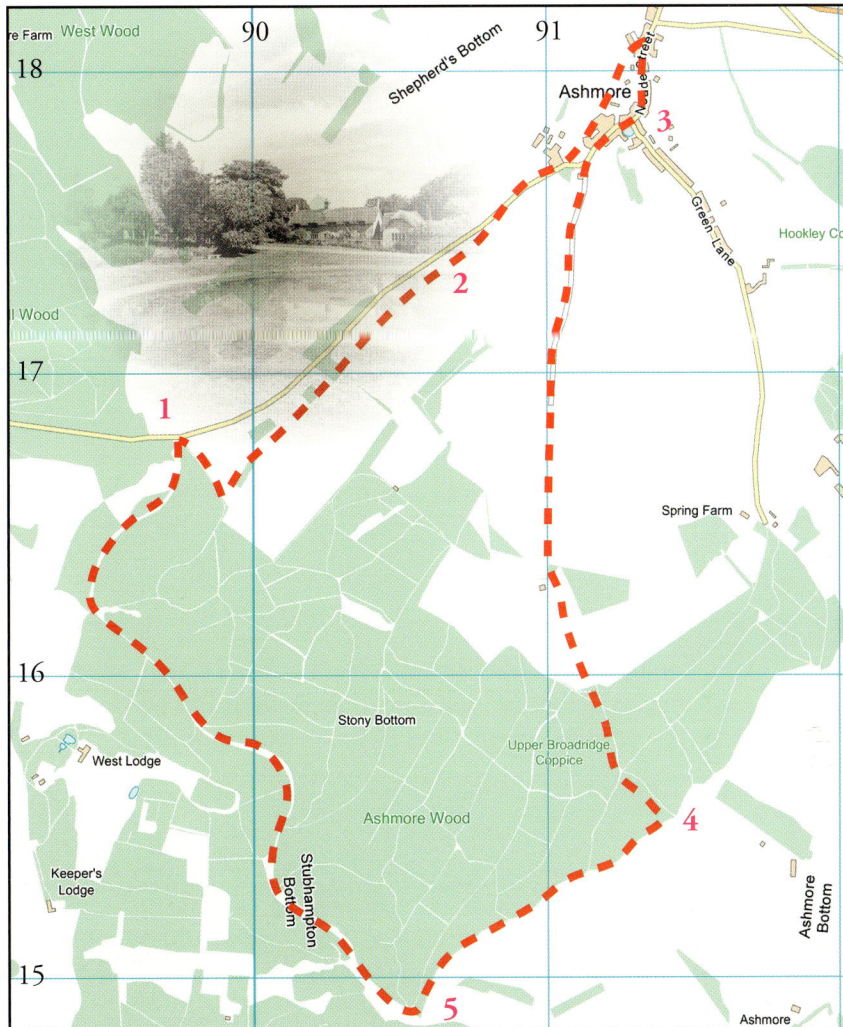

Start/parking: Ashmore Forest parking area on lane 1 mile south-west of Ashmore, ST89737 16789, SP5 5AE.

Terrain: Mainly level, one short, steep ascent. Attention needed to directions at path junctions.

Refreshments: King John Inn, Tollard Royal, 01725 516207.

Stiles: 1 **Public Toilets:** None.

Maps: OS Explorer 118; Landrangers 184 and 194.

1.   **Start ST89737 16789:** Facing the lane, turn very sharp right up a steep signed bridleway with the fence on your left. Reaching a path junction at the top of the slope, turn left through a gate and follow the upper field edges.

2.   **1 mile/1.6km ST90768 17471:** Reaching the lane, continue ahead to Manor Farm Dairy. Turn left onto the public footpath and right 50m ahead. Follow the footpath behind the church. Exit via a stile. Follow the path ahead through gates. Turn sharp right and follow the lane to the village pond.

3.   **1¾ miles/2.9km ST91291 17782:** Take the lane south-west past the church. Turn left onto a broad stony track signed "Ashmore Wood". Ignore side turnings. Continue ahead at signs for "Ashmore Wood", then "Great Peaky Coppice".

4.   **3½ miles/5.5km ST91441 15534:** At a T junction of paths at the far side of Ashmore Wood, turn right "Great Peaky Coppice" on the Wessex Ridgeway.

5.   **4 miles/6.5km ST90543 14877:** Reaching a junction of four paths, turn right and keep the fence on your left until you reach a path division at a metal gate. Do not turn uphill, but keep right along the level bridleway. Ignore the Stony Bottom turning. Continue ahead at the following track junctions through Stubhampton Bottom. Ignore side paths. Follow the main track to the start.

This pleasing walk explores the fields and woodland of Cranborne Chase with fine views over rolling chalk hills and valleys. One of Dorset's most attractive villages, Ashmore is also its highest at 219m (over 700ft) and is clustered around its clay lined pond, a magnet for dragonflies and birds.

The village pond at Ashmore.

There was a prehistoric burial mound (barrow) at Washer's Pit (Point 1) until it was flattened to make way for a road in 1840. Before that, locals reported the sounds of "gabbygammies", unearthly spirits that made equally unearthly noises. These ghostly sounds ceased when the barrow was levelled and its remains buried in the village churchyard. Perhaps the ancient spirits are now at rest?

Washer's Pit, now a small marshy area and formerly a well, is said to be haunted by a spectral white lady. One night the cook from the nearby big house had a prophetic dream about the well. She rode out and found a lady, dressed in white, hanging there from an ash tree.

Sixpenny Handley and Bottlebush Down - *a phantom horseman*

Distance: 8¾ miles/13.8km Time: 4½ hours Grade: Challenging

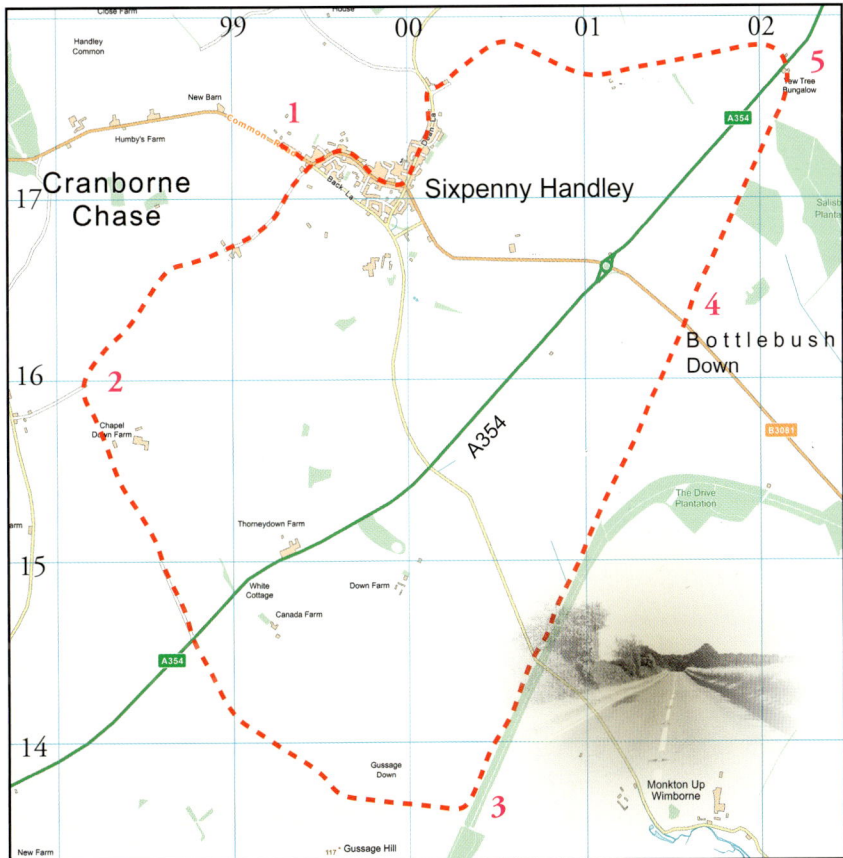

Start/parking: Sixpenny Handley Recreation Ground ST99283 17393, SP5 5NJ.
Terrain: Gently undulating. Paths and bridleways, mainly signed.
Refreshments: The Penny Tap (in Sports Pavilion) at start.
Stiles: 4 **Public Toilets:** None.
Maps: OS Explorer 118 (north sheet); Landrangers 184 and 195.

1.   **Start ST99283 17393:** Turn left towards the village. Turn right opposite the school by Park Cottage into a stony track. Reaching a gate, bear left between fences on a bridleway. Ignore the footpath left. Continue to a crosstracks.

2.   **1½ miles/2.3km ST98163 15992:** Turn left "Jubilee Trail". Follow it to the A354. Cross carefully. Continue ahead on the signed bridleway. This cuts through the Dorset Cursus. Continuing over Gussage Down, the track passes several long barrows and an ancient settlement. Continue ahead over two crosstracks.

3.   **3¾ miles5.9km SU00200 13542:** Reaching a line of trees, turn left onto the signed bridleway. You are now on Ackling Dyke. Follow the track ahead through trees and over a lane. Look out for more tumuli. Continue over the Cursus to the supposedly haunted B3081.

4.   **5½ miles/8.8km SU01575 16319:** Cross the road carefully and follow the verge left for 25m. Cross the stile and continue along Ackling Dyke. Bottlebush Down is on your right. Look out for more tumuli ahead on your left. The last part of the path is rather overgrown. Use the field edge on the right, being careful to respect growing crops.

5.   **6½miles/10.3km   SU02206 17668:** Reaching a crosstrack, turn left and walk behind the building (a garage). Cross the road carefully and follow the bridleway ahead, keeping the field edge on your right. Cross a track and continue ahead on a grassy path and then an enclosed track. Cross a lane. Follow the path ahead. Keep right when the path divides. Continue ahead at the next path junction. Walk through the campsite to the lane. Turn right. Follow the lane right by the school to the start.

Previous page: Ackling Dyke, the best preserved Roman road in southern England. Above: Bronze Age burial barrows near Ackling Dyke.

This stimulating walk explores high downland and has a good deal of histori-cal interest, including one of Dorset's best groupings of "barrows", ancient burial mounds. Long barrows date back to the Neolithic, more than 2500 BC, while round barrows were the work of Bronze Age peoples between 2500 and 800 BC.

For three miles we walk Ackling Dyke, a Roman road which ran in a straight line, 22 miles from Old Sarum (Salisbury) to Badbury Rings hillfort (page 33). Much of it still exists as an embankment up to 50ft wide and 6ft high – a clear statement of power. On this walk it twice crosses the Dorset Cursus, a Neolithic earthwork of parallel banks, which runs 6¼ miles over the downs. Its purpose is a mystery: it may have been connected with rites of passage, with ancestor veneration or acted as a boundary, perhaps to a ceremonial landscape. The Cursus has mainly been revealed through aerial photography and crop marks.

A Phantom Horseman

Bottlebush Down (Point 4) is haunted by a phantom horseman, as reported by an archaeologist, Dr Clay, in 1924. One evening, he was driving along the B3081 when he saw a horseman riding hell for leather towards him. Clay slowed his car to let the horseman pass, but the rider turned his horse to gal-lop beside the car.

Clay wrote: "I could see that he was no ordinary horseman, for he had bare legs, and wore a long loose cloak. His horse had a long mane and tail, but I could see neither bridle nor stirrup. His face was turned towards me, but I could not see his features. He seemed to be threatening me with some implement, which he waved in his right hand above his head."

After riding beside the car for some 300 feet, the horseman vanished beside a round barrow. Clay returned many times to reassure himself that this had been some trick of the fading light, but abandoned his scepticism when a local shepherd claimed he too had seen the phantom horseman and two young women told how they were severely frightened by the armed rider as they cycled over Bottlebush Down.

Bibliography, Further Reading and websites

Osborn, George, *Dorset Curiosities*, Dovecote Press, Dorset, 1986. Accessible miscellany of curious Dorset sites.
Hesketh, Robert, *Legends and Folklore of Dorset*, Inspiring Places Publishing, Fordingbridge, 2013. Companion to this collection.
Udal, John Symonds, *Dorsetshire Folk-lore*, first published 1922, second edition by Toucan Press, Guernsey, 1970. Still the definitive guide to Dorset's mysteries and folklore.
Underwood, Peter, *Ghosts of Dorset*, Bossiney Books, Launceston, 2006. Well written account by an acknowledged authority on the paranormal.
Westwood, Robert, *Mysterious Places of Dorset*, Inspiring Places Publishing, Fordingbridge, 2007. Companion to this collection.

www.darkdorset.co.uk - A rich trove of informative articles on folklore, customs, legends, ghosts and more.
www.paranormaldatabase.com - Rich source of information on the supernatural in Britain.
www.mysteriousbritain.co.uk - Useful national database.
www.stoneseeker.net - Site dedicated to Dorset's ancient mysteries.

Front cover: Ackling Dyke Roman road and Ashmore village pond.
Rear cover: Badbury Rings.
All photographs by the author except pg 2, pg 41 top right, pg 42 and inside rear cover by Robert Westwood.